What Should I Wear?

by Frank Hartley

NATIONAL GEOGRAPHIC LEARNING |  CENGAGE

Everyone has favorite clothes. What clothes do you like to wear to school?

How do you decide what to wear?

Which clothes are dirty?
Which clothes are clean?

Some people need to wear special clothes for their job.

A spacesuit helps an astronaut breathe in space.

A beekeeper wears a special veil on his head. The veil protects him from angry bees.

These clothes might save a life!

A stunt performer wears padded clothes and a helmet for protection.

Firefighters wear special coats and pants called *turnouts*. These clothes don't catch fire easily, and they are waterproof, too.

Other people wear clothes that look the same every day.

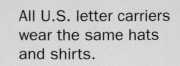

All U.S. letter carriers wear the same hats and shirts.

Clothes make these people easy to recognize.

Employees at some stores wear the same colors.

Many people dress up for festivals and holidays.

An Indian bride wears a fancy dress. The dress is called a *lehnga*. An Indian groom wears a fancy coat. The coat is called a *sherwani*.

During Kwanzaa, men and women wear African shirts. These shirts are called *kaftans*.

Special clothes help people celebrate their culture.

These boys and girls wear Polish folk costumes. They perform Polish dances.

These people wear colors of the Puerto Rican flag. They watch the Puerto Rican Day Parade in New York City.

Some athletes wear clothes for good luck!

Tiger Woods wears a red shirt when he plays golf on Sundays.

Can clothes bring good luck? Who knows?

Michael Jordan wore his lucky shorts under his Chicago Bulls uniform. He led his team to six NBA championships.

We choose our clothes for many different reasons—including just for fun!